Electing the President

By Peter Finn

Published in 2025 by Cavendish Square Publishing, LLC
2544 Clinton Street Buffalo, NY 14224

Website: cavendishsq.com

Library of Congress Cataloging-in-Publication Data

Names: Finn, Peter, 1978- author.
Title: Electing the president / Peter Finn.
Description: Buffalo, New York : Cavendish Square Publishing, 2025. |
Series: The inside guide. U.S. government leaders | Includes index.
Identifiers: LCCN 2024000014 (print) | LCCN 2024000015 (ebook) | ISBN 9781502671523 (library binding) | ISBN 9781502671516 (paperback) | ISBN 9781502671530 (ebook)
Subjects: LCSH: Presidents–United States–Election–Juvenile literature. | Elections–United States–Juvenile literature. | Electoral college–United States–Juvenile literature.
Classification: LCC JK528 .F56 2025 (print) | LCC JK528 (ebook) | DDC 324.973–dc23/eng/20240108
LC record available at https://lccn.loc.gov/2024000014
LC ebook record available at https://lccn.loc.gov/2024000015

Editor: Therese Shea
Copyeditor: Michele Suchomel-Casey
Designer: Deanna Lepovich

The photographs in this book are used by permission and through the courtesy of: Cover Joseph Sohm/Shutterstock.com; p. 4 Victorian Traditions/Shutterstock.com; p. 6 TREKPix/Shutterstock.com; pp. 7 (left and right), 19, 20 Courtesy of the Library of Congress; p. 8 (top) Evan El-Amin/Shutterstock.com; p. 8 (bottom) Consolidated News Photos/Shutterstock.com; p. 10 (top and bottom) vectorfusionart/Shutterstock.com; p. 12 miker/Shutterstock.com; p. 13 Emily O Ross/Shutterstock.com; p. 14 Iowa Caucus Precinct 15 in Ames (2020) During First Alignment/Wikimedia Commons; p. 15 Gregory Reed/Shutterstock.com; p. 16 Nicole Glass Photography/Shutterstock.com; p. 18 Aaron of L.A. Photography/Shutterstock.com; p. 21 President George H. W. Bush and President-Elect Bill Clinton/Wikimedia Commons; p. 22 Rawpixel.com/Shutterstock.com; p. 24 AtlasbyAtlas Studio/Shutterstock.com; p. 25 Rena Schild/Shutterstock.com; p. 26 Rob Crandall/Alamy Stock Photo; p. 27 P20210120CK-1111 (50912592147)/Wikimedia Commons; p. 29 (left) HOMONSTOCK/Shutterstock.com; p. 29 (right) Hethers/Shutterstock.com.

CPSIA compliance information: Batch #CSCSQ25: For further information contact Cavendish Square Publishing LLC at 1-877-980-4450.

Printed in the United States of America

CONTENTS

George Washington was the first elected president under the U.S. Constitution.

Chapter One

HAIL TO THE CHIEF

Countries around the world have different kinds of leaders. Some have monarchs, such as kings and queens. Others have a prime minister, an official who works with a lawmaking body such as a parliament. In 1787, the Founding Fathers of the United States declared the head of state for their new nation would be a president. The president is elected by U.S. voters to serve a four-year term in office. They can only serve for two terms at most.

The president is in charge of the executive branch of the federal government, which is the part of the government that enforces the laws of the nation. As head of the executive branch, the president is the commander in chief of the U.S. armed forces. The Federal Bureau of Investigation (FBI) and Central Intelligence Agency (CIA) are considered part of this branch too. Other official offices within this branch of government oversee parks, collect taxes, and make sure food and water supplies are safe.

Fast Fact

The U.S. Postal Service and National Aeronautics and Space Administration (NASA) are part of the executive branch of the U.S. government.

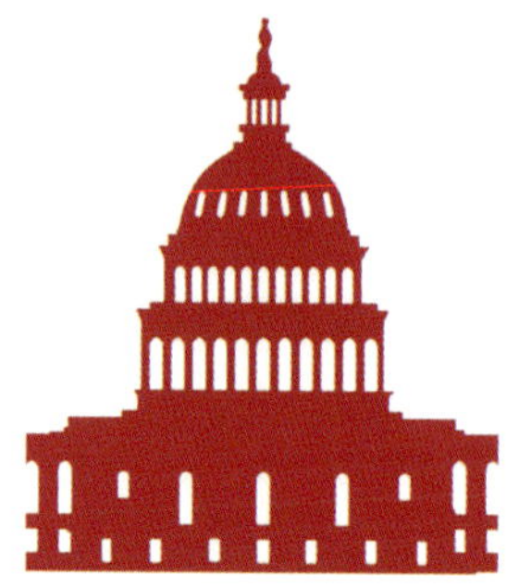

LEGISLATIVE **EXECUTIVE** **JUDICIAL**

makes laws *carries out laws* *evaluates laws*

The executive, legislative, and judicial branches of the federal government each have their own powers as well as the ability to check the powers of the other two branches.

What Makes a Good President?

U.S. presidents usually have certain qualities that make them good for the job. Confidence, honesty, and responsibility are important parts of a good leader's character. Voters want to elect people who have proven they'll carry through with their promises. A good leader can make hard decisions when they need to, but they also listen to experts' opinions and weigh decisions for the good of the nation. Most presidents are good public speakers who can convey their ideas well.

Fast Fact

John F. Kennedy was the youngest president elected to office. He was 43 when he was elected in 1960. Theodore Roosevelt was 42 when he became president, after President William McKinley was assassinated in 1901.

Not all presidents have had all these qualities, however.

There are a few requirements that a candidate for president must have, according to the U.S. Constitution. For example, only a person who's a natural-born citizen may be president. They must have lived in the United States for at least 14 years. A presidential candidate must be at least 35 years old too. Both men and women may become president.

Fast Fact

A natural-born citizen is one who has been a U.S. citizen from the time of their birth. This term is used in the Constitution.

Preparing for Politics

Presidents have come from a variety of backgrounds. Some, such as George Washington, were rich, but others, such as Abraham Lincoln,

As of 2023, 25 presidents have practiced law, and at least 10 were teachers. Father and son presidents John Adams and John Quincy Adams were lawyers and teachers at different times in their lives.

John Adams

John Quincy Adams

Donald Trump

Joe Biden

Among recent presidents, Donald Trump had been a businessperson and TV producer before becoming president. Joe Biden had been a U.S. senator and U.S. vice president.

GETTING AROUND

Running a presidential campaign is a bit like selling a candidate to voters. For months—and sometimes years—candidates travel the country to tell people what they'll do if elected. Candidates give speeches, do interviews, and hold rallies. They may visit places such as nursing homes and factories to meet voters. An important part of a campaign is advertising. From TV and newspaper ads to mailers and posters, candidates do their best to make their name as recognizable to voters as they can. Today, all candidates have websites and use social media sites such as Facebook and X (formerly known as Twitter) to reach voters.

came from poorer beginnings. Presidents have been farmers, military leaders, teachers, a university president, and a geologist. Most have a background in politics, or government, and law.

All Americans who want to become president have ideas about how the federal government should work. However, they need more than ideas to run for U.S. president. They need the support of many, many people. They also need money so they can travel and campaign. The road to the presidency is a long, expensive, tiring one, but one that many politicians wish to walk.

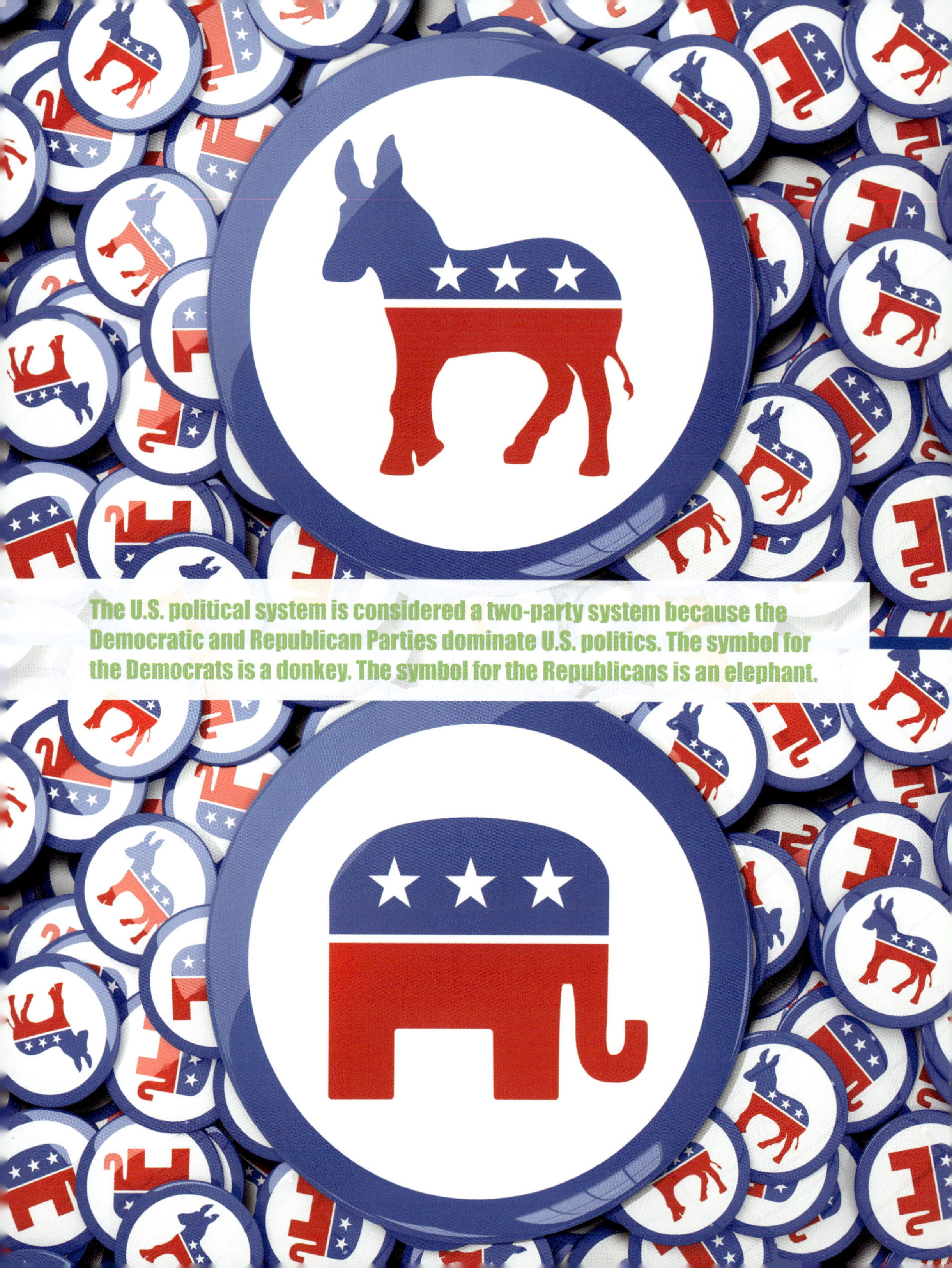

The U.S. political system is considered a two-party system because the Democratic and Republican Parties dominate U.S. politics. The symbol for the Democrats is a donkey. The symbol for the Republicans is an elephant.

PARTIES AND PRIMARIES

The only president who didn't belong to a political party was George Washington. Every president since has had the support and **endorsement** of a political party. Some of these parties—such as the Democratic-Republicans and the Whigs—are no longer in existence. Today, the United States has two major political parties: the Democrats and the Republicans. While it's not required that a presidential candidate belong to one of these two parties, the support of a major political party gives a candidate more resources—including money—to reach more voters, among other advantages.

Political parties other than the Democratic and Republican Parties are called third parties. These are smaller organizations that often focus on just a few issues. The Green Party's main interest is protecting Earth and its natural resources, for example. As of 2023, no third-party candidate has won the presidency, however. In fact, no third-party presidential candidate has won in a U.S. state in more than 50 years.

Fast Fact

A political party is an group of people who share similar ideas about how their government should be run.

Picking a Candidate

Several people from a political party may want to be president. To be an

The Libertarian Party, whose members support individual rights over government authority, is the third largest political party in the United States.

official candidate on a voting **ballot**, a person must have enough party members sign a **petition** of support. Then, candidates compete state by state for their party's nomination for president.

Some states hold elections called primaries before the national election, while other states have meetings called caucuses. A caucus is a system of local meetings where voters decide which candidate to support by different means—from secret ballots to forming groups for each candidate and trying to convince other voters to join their group. A primary is a statewide voting process in which voters choose their favorite candidate. Primaries and caucuses are held in the winter or spring before the presidential election in November.

Fast Fact

Some primaries and caucuses are open to all voters, while some require that voters be registered with a particular political party.

At both primaries and caucuses, candidates are awarded delegates if they do well in the final counts. These

Caucuses were the first method at the state level for choosing presidential candidates. Primaries were introduced in the early 1900s.

THE IOWA CAUCUSES

The Iowa caucuses are arguably the most famous caucuses. They occur in school gyms, libraries, and even homes. In the Iowa Republican caucuses, a vote is taken for a candidate among all gathered participants. In the Democratic caucuses, participants gather in groups according to the candidate they support. Undecided voters gather in a group too. Candidates or supporters speak to the groups. A count of each group is taken and reported. Supporters of candidates who don't receive 15 percent of the total vote at the caucus need to join another group. This is called realignment. A final count is then taken. Through conventions that follow, delegates for the winning candidates are chosen for the national convention.

Participants at the 2020 Iowa caucuses join another candidate's group after their candidate didn't receive the required number of votes.

Fast Fact

Primaries and caucuses are held well before the national convention, and one candidate often ends up being the only person left in the race by then.

A party's national convention is an opportunity for a candidate to address the entire nation for the first time as the official nominee of a political party.

delegates, who are usually people of some importance in their state political party or early supporters of a candidate, go on to vote for a candidate at their party's national **convention**.

Some delegates must vote for the winner of the primary or caucus. Others have the freedom to vote for the candidate of their choice. Rules for this depend on the political party and the state. The results of the votes at the political party's national convention determine the nominee—the candidate who will represent the party in the national election, called the general election.

Undecided voters may vote for a presidential candidate who has a running mate they admire. Presidential candidate Joe Biden chose Senator Kamala Harris as his running mate.

THE JOURNEY TO THE GENERAL ELECTION

With their selection as their political party's nominee, a presidential candidate begins their campaign for the general election. One of the most important decisions they make at this point is their running mate—the person who will be their vice president if elected. The main duty of the vice president of the United States is to be ready to take on the role of president if the president dies or resigns. As of 2023, eight vice presidents have become president when the sitting president died. Gerald Ford was the only vice president to gain the office because of a president resigning, which Richard Nixon did in 1974.

Debates

Presidential candidates want voters' attention so they can win them over with their ideas. They want to look more **competent** than their opponents. One of the ways they can accomplish both these goals is to take part in **debates** with their opponents.

> **Fast Fact**
>
> Kamala Harris, President Joe Biden's vice president, was the first female, Black American, and Asian American to serve as U.S. vice president.

John F. Kennedy and Richard Nixon had the

Debates between candidates of the same party take place before primaries and caucuses.

Fast Fact

As of 2023, the most-watched presidential debate took place in 2016. About 84 million people watched the debate between Democratic candidate Hillary Clinton and Republican candidate Donald Trump.

first televised presidential debate in 1960. Since then, the main candidates hold two or three debates that are widely seen on TV. This is a chance for voters to see how the candidates' views and ideas may differ. Sometimes debates have a theme, such as foreign policy. While neither candidate is officially declared a winner at a debate, voters often have an opinion about which one presented themself best.

Richard Nixon (*left*) was the vice president at the time of his debates with Senator John F. Kennedy (*right*). Nixon lost the presidential election of 1960 to Kennedy but was later elected in 1968.

Some think that presidential debates on TV forever changed U.S. elections. A candidate's appearance became as important as their ideas. Vice presidential candidates also take part in debates with each other.

Fast Fact

Before television, presidential candidates sometimes campaigned by train. Harry S. Truman, who served as president from 1945 to 1953, spent 8 weeks on a train traveling to 28 states.

Keeping Promises

Candidates have ideas about what they'd like to do as president. They repeat these ideas during the debates and in the many speeches they give throughout their campaign. It's important for candidates to

PRESIDENTIAL SLOGANS

Often, a presidential campaign uses red, white, and blue colors or symbols like the U.S. flag, an eagle, or the Liberty Bell. This is supposed to send the message that the candidate is a person who loves the United States deeply. In addition, the campaign often uses catchy slogans, or short messages to represent their values and aims. Presidential slogans go back in U.S. election history to at least 1840. Donald Trump's 2016 campaign slogan was "Make America Great Again," and in his failed 2020 campaign it was "Keep America Great." Joe Biden's 2020 campaign used the slogan "Build Back Better," and for 2024 it was "Let's Finish the Job."

In 1840, William Henry Harrison and John Tyler's election campaign used the slogan "Tippecanoe and Tyler Too." (Tippecanoe refers to Harrison's military victory over Native Americans in 1811.)

George H. W. Bush (*right*) is shown with President-elect Bill Clinton after the 1992 election.

choose their messages carefully. They may be what get them elected, but campaign promises need to be achievable too.

When George H. W. Bush ran for president in 1988, he made a promise in a speech: "Read my lips: no new taxes." It was a popular message at the time and helped him defeat Democratic candidate Michael Dukakis. However, during his term, Bush realized new taxes were needed. When he ran for reelection in 1992, his words were used against him. Some voters were angry he had broken his promise and didn't vote for him again. He lost to Democratic candidate Bill Clinton.

Voter turnout can play a big part in an election's outcome. A presidential candidate who inspires a particular group of people to vote may have an edge on Election Day.

FROM ELECTION TO INAUGURATION

As Election Day gets closer, candidates spend more time in states where the outcome is uncertain. These are often called swing states since the election can swing to either the Democratic or Republican candidate. (Other states historically vote for either the Democratic or Republican candidate in overwhelming numbers.)

Some organizations put together **polls** to see how each candidate is doing. Candidates use polling information to better target their campaign. For example, a poll may reveal that a candidate is popular with men over age 35, but not with women in the same age group. To better reach this group, the candidate may hold an event or release an ad targeted at women.

Fast Fact

States choose electors for the Electoral College. In many states, the state political party selects them. The Constitution says electors can't be members of Congress or federal employees.

The Electoral College

There are two votes to watch in U.S. presidential elections: the popular vote and the electoral vote. Together, they determine the winner. The popular vote is the number of votes cast by all voters. The electoral vote is cast by representatives from each state called electors. These electors are part of a process called the Electoral College, which was established in the U.S. Constitution.

To become president, a candidate needs to win the most electoral votes. Since there are 538 members of Congress, there are 538 electoral votes (and electors). A candidate needs to win at least one more than half this number, or 270, to be elected president. In most states, the candidate who receives

Fast Fact

In most states, the electors must vote for the winner of the state's popular vote. States threaten "faithless electors" with fines or other punishments.

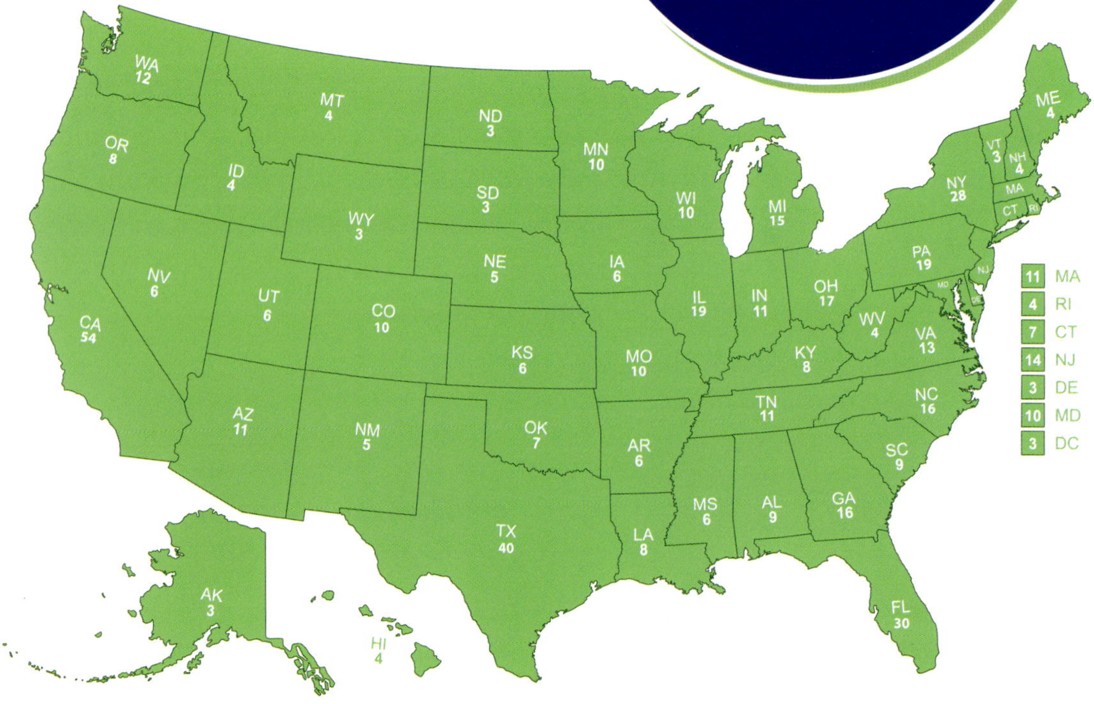

Each state has a number of electoral votes equal to its number of congressmembers. In addition, Washington, D.C., has three electors.

the most popular votes receives all the electoral votes from that state. (So, voters are actually voting for the electors for their chosen candidate.)

Some people would like to end the Electoral College. Others support it because it gives smaller, less populated states more of a say in elections.

The Job Begins

After a candidate wins the general election, they're known as the president-elect. The president-elect begins to choose people for key government positions, including their **cabinet**. The team of people who helped the

THE COURT DECIDED

Usually, the presidential candidate who wins both the popular vote and the electoral vote takes office. Five times in U.S. history, the candidate who won the popular vote didn't win enough electoral votes to be elected. The 2000 election results between Al Gore and George W. Bush were very close, so close that the election came down to the votes in one state: Florida. After a recount, Bush was declared the winner in Florida, giving him the needed electoral votes overall. However, many ballots had been set aside as they hadn't been marked clearly, so Gore protested. The election decision went to the U.S. Supreme Court, which named Bush the winner.

In 2000, Al Gore won the nation's popular vote by more than 500,000 votes but lost the electoral vote to George W. Bush. People are shown here demonstrating in front of the U.S. Supreme Court Building in 2000.

Fast Fact

In 2016, Donald Trump defeated Hillary Clinton, winning 304 electoral votes overall. However, Clinton had received 2.8 million more popular votes than Trump.

president get elected often becomes part of the staff at the White House too.

The new president's **inauguration** typically takes place on January 20 following the election. During the ceremony, the president takes the oath of the office as stated in the Constitution: "I do solemnly swear (or affirm) that I will faithfully execute the office of President of the United States, and will to the best of my ability, preserve, protect and defend the Constitution of the United States."

Over the next four years, the president will enforce the laws of the country and represent the nation around the world. As the time nears for another presidential election, they'll decide whether to run again. If they do, they'll be the **incumbent** candidate. They need to campaign again. They may be reelected if American voters approve of their presidency.

The inauguration of the U.S. president takes place at the U.S. Capitol.

MORE PRESIDENTIAL ELECTION HISTORY

1789

George Washington becomes the only president ever to receive all of the electoral votes.

1800

Thomas Jefferson and his running mate, Aaron Burr, tie in the election. The election is decided in Jefferson's favor by the House of Representatives. (Later, the 12th **Amendment** requires separate votes cast for presidents and vice presidents.)

1860

Abraham Lincoln is the first Republican elected U.S. president.

1912

During a campaign event, Theodore Roosevelt is shot. The bullet is stopped by a 50-page speech in his pocket. Roosevelt continues speaking after the shooting.

1944

Franklin D. Roosevelt is elected to his fourth presidential term. (An amendment later limits presidential terms to two.)

1974

Gerald Ford is the only president and vice president to never be elected. Ford becomes vice president when Vice President Spiro Agnew resigns in 1973 and president when Nixon resigns in 1974.

2008

Barack Obama becomes the first Black American elected president in U.S. history and serves two terms.

2016

Hillary Clinton becomes the first woman to be a major political party's candidate for U.S. president.

THINK ABOUT IT!

1. What is your opinion of the Electoral College's role in presidential elections?
2. Do you think presidents should be limited to two terms? Why or why not?
3. Do you think the current voting age of 18 should be raised, be lowered, or remain the same? Why?
4. Do you think the process for presidential candidates getting elected should be changed in any way? Explain.

GLOSSARY

amendment: A change or addition to a constitution.

assassinate: To kill someone, especially a public figure.

ballot: A listing of candidates' names used for voting.

cabinet: A group of senior officials appointed by the president as special advisers.

competent: Having the right abilities or qualities for a job.

convention: A gathering of people who have a common interest or purpose.

debate: A formal argument or public discussion.

endorsement: The act of officially supporting or approving of someone.

inauguration: A ceremony marking the start of someone's term in public office.

incumbent: A person who presently holds an office or position.

petition: A written request signed by many people.

poll: The process and result of asking questions to find out what most people think of something or someone. Also, a place where votes are cast.